GW00359753

PLAY

JOHNS HOPKINS
UNIVERSITY PRESS

AARHUS UNIVERSITY PRESS

MARC MALMDORF ANDERSEN

PLAY

© Marc Malmdorf Andersen
and Johns Hopkins University Press 2022
Layout and cover: Camilla Jørgensen, Trefold
Cover photograph: Poul Ib Henriksen
Publishing editor: Søren Mogensen Larsen
Translated from the Danish by Heidi Flegal
Printed by Narayana Press, Denmark
Printed in Denmark 2022

ISBN 978-1-4214-4484-0 (pbk)
ISBN 978-1-4214-4485-7 (ebook)

Library of Congress Control Number: 2022930095

*Special discounts are available for bulk purchases of this
book. For more information, please contact Special Sales at
specialsales@jh.edu.*

Published in the United States by:

Johns Hopkins University Press
2715 North Charles Street
Baltimore, MD 21218-4363
www.press.jhu.edu

Published with the generous support of the
Aarhus University Research Foundation and
the Danish Arts Foundation

Purchase in Denmark: ISBN 978-87-7219-187-4

Aarhus University Press
Finlandsgade 29
8200 Aarhus N
Denmark
www.aarhusuniversitypress.dk

CONTENTS

THE EVOLUTION OF PLAY

MY KINGDOM FOR A STRAW

"Daddy, I need a straw, 'cause the only thing anybody ever drinks on Atecopia is coconut water. Atecopia, that's our island, Daddy, and we always drink coconut water here. It has to be a purple straw. And I'm Princess of Atecopia, so will you be the king, Daddy? ... No, you can't be the prince, 'cause there *is* no prince on Atecopia, so you can only be King. Now you have to sit on that chair – that's *your* throne. And the chair next to it is *my* throne. So we can sit right here and drink coconut water. And let's pretend Eva's our dog! She's too little to be a princess like me."

This is the older of my two daughters having fun. Every day she and her sister – they were five and two when she said this – make me a front-row spectator to some of the countless types of play children come up with. When she carefully arranges Atecopia's sparkling treasures, she is quiet as a mouse. When she invades the neighbouring kingdom, foam sword held high, the whole house shakes.

As she hosts a royal party, filling her throne room with song and dance, she is rhythm from head to toe. When she describes the marvellous creatures she can see from her castle turret, her imagination is in overdrive. If she plays with friends at our house as the Princess of Atecopia, with her faithful, playdough-munching dog in tow, she might throw a royal tea party for her guests. But she can also play alone, addressing her invisible subjects from the top bunk bed like an empress.

The term 'play' refers to a huge variety of different activities. When we play, we develop trust and intimacy, solve problems and explore. We train motor skills, decode symbols, think creatively and perform complex social interactions. Even so, children and adults across the globe instinctively recognise playful behaviour as soon as they see it, and every known culture in the world has a word for this peculiar type of behaviour.

THE GORDIAN KNOT OF EVOLUTIONARY BIOLOGY

Ever since the English naturalist Charles Darwin published his groundbreaking work *On the Origin of Species* in 1859, scientists and researchers have used natural and sexual selection to explain all sorts of physical characteristics and behaviours in humans and other animals. Darwin demonstrated how, through evolution, species have adapted in various ways to promote their survival and procreation.

The hippopotamus, for instance, is so aggressive that even crocodiles stay away, while the hare has developed reaction patterns that make it dash off at the faintest hint of danger. These are two very different ways of getting by in the world, yet both are extremely effective.

Now consider peacocks, which for eons have adapted so as to attract the opposite sex more effectively. Because of peahens' age-old preference for big, gorgeous tails, peacocks have developed disproportionately large show-stopping, shimmering, greenish-blue fans twice their body length. This is impractical when hungry predators are on the prowl, yet peafowl have survived, so their showy-tail strategy obviously worked.

When it comes to play, evolutionary biologists have struggled since Darwin's day, for play is an odd behaviour, expending energy but serving no obvious function for survival or reproduction. Why do lion cubs opt for a scuffle in the heat instead of napping under a shady tree? Why do young elephants love to chase birds and other small animals when they could spend their time foraging? Why do young bonobos dangle high in the treetops, gripped firmly by older ape-clan members but still risking injury or death if they plummet to the forest floor?

Despite this apparent lack of purpose, most biologists assume that play – a high-energy, high-risk behaviour – must serve some crucial function. If not, it is hard to explain why so many intelligent species have developed play as part of their behavioural repertoire. But how, then, does play increase the chances of survival or reproduction? How do baby rats benefit from play-fighting? And what do young Hawaiian crows get out of picking up twigs in their beaks, shaking them and tossing them around?

8

Most scientists believe that while its value is not always immediately evident, play enables humans and other animals to learn and master routines that will be important in their later lives. It can strengthen physical or social skills, for example, or help creatures explore and learn about their environment. In short, play helps young individuals become better adults.

NO FOOD AND NO PLAY
MAKES KNUT A DULL BEAR

In their 2013 book entitled *Play, Playfulness, Creativity and Innovation*, the British biologists Patrick Bateson and Paul Martin present five characteristics of play.

First, play is inherently fun and rewarding. This sets it apart from other types of human and animal behaviour that are mainly aimed at obtaining some form of reward *afterwards*. People go to work because they want to get paid. Lions hunt gazelles because they are hungry and want to eat. Stags spar because they want to mate with a herd of hinds. Not so with play, which animals and humans spontaneously engage in simply because it is fun. Evidently, the act of playing is a reward in itself.

Second, play is not serious. When dogs, rats or elephants play-fight, they are not trying to hurt their opponent. And when children pretend to throw a scoop of ice cream, eggs and pasta into a frying pan in their toy kitchen, they are not really trying to make something to eat. Play appears to have no immediate practical purpose, which is also why humans and animals often take great pains to signal 'now we are just playing'. This prevents playmates from misunderstanding the situation. A dog, for instance, will often invite other dogs to play by stretching its forelegs to the ground, leaning on its elbows and lifting its rear end and tail. This way its playfellows know that their boisterous play will all be in good fun – no hard biting allowed.

Third, play is innovative and a generator of novelty. Just think of how small children, often to their parents' dismay, investigate a multitude of ways to use porridge – besides eating it, of course. Or think of a mature, responsible father who suddenly, willingly, finds himself obeying the every whim of a five-year-old self-proclaimed princess of Atecopia.

Fourth, play looks different. This is why animals and people so easily recognise play when they see it. Play is often repetitive, with minor variations in each repetition. Anyone who has played peekaboo with a child knows that to keep the child's interest, the game must balance repetitiveness with gradual developments. New twists and surprises must slowly be introduced, such as changes to voice inflection or props.

Play is also recognisable because it often borrows actions and thoughts from daily life and distorts or exaggerates them, or leaves out certain things. Rats fighting in earnest usually bite their opponent's flanks, whereas play-fighting rats just nose and push at each other's necks and shoulders.

Fifth and finally, play is a sign of well-being and only occurs in the absence of illness, hunger and stress. In December 2017, many were riveted by the media coverage of a starving polar bear on Baffin Island in Canada, half-dead and desperate to find food. A polar bear in that condition would never play – but might after its basic needs had been met. Animals that are cold, hungry, sick or frightened do not play. A continent away, at the Berlin Zoo, the delightful hand-raised polar bear Knut (2006–2011, RIP) would often play with his ball or wrestle with his keeper. We play when we feel good.

SPECIALISED HENS AND VERSATILE CROWS

Play is not for everyone. On the contrary, it is primarily observed in intelligent, warm-blooded creatures. Mammals like monkeys, dogs, pigs, cats, elephants, horses, bears, otters and humans play, and so do whales and dolphins, as well as parrots and crows. Simply put, animals with a relatively long childhood play the most, and these particular species often have larger brains than other animals and are better at learning. This is one of the reasons why most play scientists and scholars believe play and learning are intimately linked. The academic consensus is that play is a behaviour that enables young animals to explore and learn about their physical and social environment.

And young animals take their play seriously. A scientific experiment conducted in 1990 by the South African biologist and geneticist David Wood-Gush and his colleagues showed that when piglets kept alone in an empty pen were given access to a new, exciting pen next door, they would play longer than piglets from pens that already had sticks, stones and logs to play with.

Similarly, compared to calves used to a free-range life, domestic calves that have been penned in will run and frolic more when the farmer finally lets them out into the meadow. In other words, animals that are prevented from playing will play *more* when the opportunity arises. The same is true of rats, which is why some scientists deliberately prevent their lab rats from playing before an experiment so they will be ready to play when they get the chance.

But why do so many species self-regulate and prioritise their play activities? Compare an ordinary chicken – an Isa Brown – with a New Caledonian crow and you will see a striking difference in their intelligence and play habits. A chicken's brain is almost fully programmed and ready to go from the moment it hatches, so that day-old chicks are able to find their own food. In fact, chickens are absolute experts at this one activity: search-and-peck foraging. They do this extremely well, but are capable of little else.

A hatchling New Caledonian crow, on the other hand, is totally helpless and can only survive if fed by adults. It is one of the few bird species which, as it matures, begins to play. Once it can fly it tries out various aerial acrobatics, flying upside down and doing somersaults in mid-air, and when grooming in water it often splashes about long after it is clean. Young crows are especially fond of long, thin twigs, which they pick up in their beaks, shake and toss around. And adults often throw twigs to juniors as if to encourage them to play.

Over time, young crows discover that twigs are not only fun, they are also handy for nest-building and as tools to get grubs out of deep cracks and cavities in tree bark. In this way, play enables a crow to discover a wide range of amenities and opportunities that would never cross a common chicken's mind.

TEASING OUT ANSWERS

Life as a play researcher is not always fun and games. In fact, as an academic field of study, play sometimes has us gnashing our teeth in frustration. For one thing, play is essentially a roly-poly, rough-and-tumble, sing-song, jack-in-the-box phenomenon that is extremely difficult to get a grip on. For another, play is easily confused with other phenomena that have nothing to do with it.

Different languages also have different ways of rendering the concept of play. My native language, Danish, is a case in point. Like its sister languages, Norwegian and Swedish, it has two general sets of words that cover and overlap various aspects of the extremely versatile English word 'play'. In Danish, these two sets can almost be said to represent two ends of a 'play spectrum'.

One set is based on the noun *et spil*, pronounced "it spill" and meaning 'a game', such as a card game, a board game or a computer game. The related verb is *at spille*, "at **spil**-la", which is generally used for closed-ended and rule-based activities such as playing board or computer games, or doing sports or jigsaw puzzles, where there are fixed endings and goals.

However, when a Dane uses the noun *en leg*, which is pronounced "in lie", or the related verb *at lege*, "at **lie**-ya", they are most likely referring to open-ended and unstructured forms of play with no particular goal or desired ending. You know, the sort of play where you pretend, either outdoors in a playground or indoors with things like dolls, toy cars and Lego bricks – hence the first part of that brand name.

The related nouns and verbs cannot be mixed, so Danes can *lege en leg*, or *spille et spil*, but never the twain shall meet. Amused? Bemused? Confused? Alright, enough wordplay. But you just learned why this book is called *Leg* in Danish – and hopefully you had a bit of fun yourself.

While most researchers have long suspected that play facilitates learning, only recently have we been able to accurately measure the specific benefits that people and animals get from play. In a classic school setting, measuring benefits is fairly straightforward, for instance by using baseline and year-end comparative assessments for a pupil in arithmetic. One can test the pupil with a set of problems at the beginning and the end of the year and compare the number of correct answers. The result indicates their progress for the year.

But how can a researcher measure the benefits a cat gets from playing with a ball of yarn? And how can we shed any light at all on the benefits a five-year-old girl gets from pretending to be the supreme ruler of Atecopia with her single, sporadically loyal subject?

One problem is that the variety of ways one can play is virtually infinite, as are the skills and qualities animals and humans can, or ought to, acquire to get by in the world. On top of that, sometimes the player ends up learning something very different from what would have been expected.

We know, for example, that rats that are deprived of play-fighting while growing up, but are allowed to socialise with other rats, fight just as well as rats that were allowed to play-fight. This is quite surprising, as one would expect that rats that play-fight when they are young would make better fighters later in life. Such deprived rats, when fully grown, do, however, have difficulty determining the right *timing and context* for attacking another rat. Apparently, play-fighting teaches rats more about the social rules of engagement for fights than it does about motor skills.

Another problem is that we humans have a tendency to ascribe human qualities – volition, reasoning, compassion and so on – to objects and animals that do not possess them. We shout at our computer when it crashes and beg our car to start on a frigid winter morning.

In much the same way, biologists sometimes wrongly assume that animals – say, dolphins jumping out of the water to describe a perfect curve – are playing. The reasoning seems to be that if it were a human out there, swimming, soaring and splashing about, their only reason to do so would be to play. But dolphins have many other good reasons to jump out of the water: engaging a rival, moving faster than they can underwater or simply getting rid of skin parasites by slapping down hard on the water's surface.

On the other hand, dolphins exhibit many other behaviours that can almost certainly be classified as play since they appear to have no function at all. If a large boat passes a group of dolphins, they often interrupt whatever they are doing and follow the boat to ride the bow waves, then return to the precise location and the exact same activity they had interrupted. Dolphins also sometimes use their beaks and fins to toss inedible seaweed back and forth, or they blow big rings of air bubbles from their blowholes, then try to swim through them. Presumably, the only reason they do these things is that it's really fun.

THE AGE OF EXPLORATION

SHORT ARMS, LONG FINGERS

Most people who have spent time with small children will recognise these scenarios: You look away for a moment and suddenly the little rascal has decorated the refrigerator door with lipstick, strewn the contents of your sock drawer across the floor, or re-potted your favourite houseplant in the laundry basket. Small children are incredibly curious, and they will happily play with just about anything they can get their hands on. Parents have good reason to be watchful of offspring toddling towards electrical outlets, bottles of drain cleaner or hot charcoal. They are well aware that a small child, eager to explore, knows no fear.

It is baffling that a species whose young have an incurable urge to stick their grubby little fingers – and opposable thumbs – into food processors, and indeed anything else they find interesting, has ended up dominating the planet to the degree *Homo sapiens* has. However, when a small child plays with everything it can lay its hands on, there is much more at stake than playfully passing time. They are in fact conducting a form of science.

Exploratory play is a concept in developmental psychology and biology that describes play in which humans and animals investigate physical objects: **Mama's handbag, Dada's sock drawer or a squeaky rubber doggie bone.** This is one of the first types of play we see in very young children, who, seemingly at random, investigate as much of their environment as they can, grasping at any object in reach. This type of play is common in other playful species and has even been observed in some species we do not consider playful or intelligent.

For many years, biologists have assumed that fish do not play. However, certain aquarium fish of the genus *Cichlidae* have been seen to nudge their self-righting water thermometer off kilter ten or more times in a row – even though the thermometer has no edible algae on it and the fish are showing no signs of aggression.

Another example is Kraken, perhaps the world's best-known Komodo dragon, from the Smithsonian's National Zoo in Washington, DC. In 1999 she became the object of years-long studies after the American biologist Gordon M. Burghardt decided to investigate her behaviour, having heard from her keepers that she would often push a bucket around very noisily in her enclosure.

Sometimes Kraken would also pick a keeper's pockets, once snatching a notebook and carrying it around her enclosure, but without chewing on it or otherwise damaging it. Offered various objects, she showed a preference for shoes and large plastic rings. The shoes she would bite, carry, push around and shake, often trying to put her head inside them. Scientists studied video recordings of this and noticed certain similarities with canine play – and viewed at twice normal speed, Kraken looked decidedly dog-like.

As early as the 1920s, the Swiss developmental psychologist Jean Piaget described how exploring the world could help children understand causality, although he believed they did not grasp this concept before age seven or eight. He based this belief on the wrong answers children gave him when he asked them certain questions, such as how weather phenomena arise, or how a steam engine works. You see, if you ask a five-year-old why water runs in a river, they may well answer: "So boats can sail on it." Today we know that Piaget not only drastically underestimated children's grasp of causality in the world; he also underestimated how they learn about causality through play.

INFORMATION JUNKIES

Humans love new information, and most of us are heavy consumers of broadcasts and podcasts, streamed content and multiple types of social media. Most of us also relish gossip about a neighbour's recent divorce, a manager's affair with their PA, or the mechanic down the road who, some say, is cultivating a sizable crop of interesting spiky-leafed plants in the rooms above his garage.

We love new information so much that we are often willing to ignore basic urges like hunger and fatigue if we think it might get us some juicy, intriguing or noteworthy new facts. The same is true of small children seeking data input as they unearth potted plants, pull pans from the kitchen cabinet, or take a swig of shampoo while Dada's back is turned. Children are information junkies – just like adults.

A multitude of scientific studies have documented children's thirst for new information. One had 10-month-old babies view two short videos. One video showed a toy car rolling along, then bumping into another toy car, which then started rolling. The other video was similar, but it showed the first car stopping before it bumped into the second car, which started rolling anyway. The babies often chose to spend much longer looking at video number two. They did so because it showed new, surprising information: a toy set in motion with no external impetus. To a baby, this is sensational breaking news.

It makes good sense that our attention works this way. When people or animals are hungry for new information, they learn much faster than when they are not. And as small children gradually become more mobile, they get better at finding their next data fix themselves, whether it is a lipstick in Mama's handbag or the contents of Dada's shampoo bottle.

But can children also assess the quality of the information they so enthusiastically gather? In 2007 two American developmental psychologists, Laura E. Schulz and Elizabeth Bonawitz, introduced a number of children, aged four to five, to a toy with two handles, placing it on a table between the child and the experimenter. When the experimenter pulled her handle, a little doll would pop out of the box; when the child pulled the other handle, a little duck would pop out. If both pulled their handles at the same time, the doll and duck would both pop out of the box.

The children were divided into two groups. In one group, the experimenter and the child both pulled twice, at the same time, on their handles. Then, in turn, they each pulled their own handle once. Consequently, the doll and the duck first popped out of the box twice, together; then, in turn, they each popped out of the box once. The children in this group received high-quality information about how the toy worked – seeing how one handle activated the doll and the other activated the duck.

The other group of children, in contrast, got lower-quality information. With this group, the experimenter and the child pulled their handles at the same time, three times in a row, making the doll and duck pop out of the box together each time. These children did not get a chance to work out which handle activated the doll and which activated the duck.

In all the sessions, the experimenter then took the toy, placed it out of the child's reach, and presented a new toy box that was previously unknown to the child. Next, both these toys, the old one and the new one, were placed on the table in front of the child. Then the experimenter said: "I'll be back in just a minute. Go ahead and play."

Now, which toy would the children choose to play

with, without instruction or adult supervision? The children who had received high-quality data about how the known toy worked spent more time playing with the new, unknown, interesting toy, allowing them to gather lots of new information.

However, the group of children who had received low-quality data about the first toy still found it interesting, so they continued to play with it – despite the fact that a new interesting toy was standing right next to it. This study nicely showcases how highly sensitive children are to the quality of the information they acquire during exploratory play, and how they often prefer to finish playing with things they believe can still yield new, exciting information.

"I'M GOING TO SHOW YOU HOW IT WORKS"

You may be asking yourself: Must these pint-sized vandals really be allowed to wreak havoc on their surroundings in their ceaseless quest for new information? Can we not simply tell them, or show them, the real purpose of a lipstick or a bottle of shampoo?

We certainly can, but this approach might come at a cost. In 2011, Bonawitz and her colleagues conducted another experiment, introducing four-year-olds to an odd-looking toy made of medium-sized pieces of bent, coloured plastic tubes – rather like a triple serving of the serpentine plumbing under a kitchen sink, haphazardly glued together and mounted on a wooden board.

The toy actually concealed four functions: One tube

gave a squeak when pulled on; another hid a mirror that reflected upside-down; the third tube had a button at the base that made it light up at the top; and the board had a button on it that made a little tune play.

Here, too, the children were split into two groups. With one group the experimenter brought in the toy, showed it to the child and said, "Look at my toy! This is my toy. I'm going to show you how my toy works. Watch this!" Then, a bit like a teacher – or an overly helpful, hovering father – the experimenter showed the child how to trigger the squeak by pulling on the relevant tube.

With the other group, the experimenter also brought the toy into the room with the child, but then pretended to pull, by accident, on the tube that made the toy squeak. "I just found this toy! See this toy? Huh! Did you see that? Let me try to do that." While this group also saw a demonstration of the toy's squeak function, the children received no direct instructions, unlike those in the first group.

In both groups, after the demonstration was over, the experimenter said to the child, "Wow, isn't that cool? I'm going to let you play and see if you can figure out how this toy works. Let me know when you're done." Bonawitz and her colleagues were keen to see whether the two groups of children would behave differently based on whether they had received direct instructions or not.

Not surprisingly, they found that children in both groups had quickly grasped how to make the toy squeak. And the group of children who saw the experimenter 'accidentally' activate the toy eagerly investigated the rest of it, in time discovering all four functions of the toy.

The children in the group that had been 'instructed' in the toy's function did not do this, however. They typically pulled on the tube that triggered the squeak, then did it again. And again. And again. And again. These children played for a shorter time, used fewer different types of actions and discovered fewer of the toy's functions.

In other words, the way children play is impacted by whether or not they receive adult instruction. Their play becomes more constrained, focused and narrow when adults choose to intervene and bring well-intentioned advice to the table.

This makes instruction and pedagogy a double-edged sword. It can certainly teach children about specific things and situations in the world. At the same time, it limits children's own spontaneous exploration of their surroundings, making them less inclined to discover perspectives other than the ones adults know about and show them.

BUILDING CHARACTER

LET'S PRETEND

An old proverb says that 'out of the mouth of babes' come statements that are wise, insightful or patently true, but children actually spend lots of time saying and doing things that are anything but true – not because they are intentionally lying, but because it is part of playing. You see, human children do something no other animal species seem to do – not even dolphin calves, crow fledglings or lion cubs. Children engage in rich, imaginative play. They make believe. They pretend.

But why? We know that when toddlers empty a sock drawer, paint with lipstick or hurl their porridge onto the floor, they learn about how things work and how they can manipulate objects and environments in different ways. But what do children get out of pretending to be a jockey or a chef when, in the real world, they are nowhere near a riding stable or a restaurant kitchen? And why do they pretend to be Wonder Woman, Pippi Longstocking or Batman – all fictitious characters who could never even exist in the real world? What could they possibly learn from engaging with the nonsensical, the fantastical and the unreal?

As early as age one, children begin to pretend that

things are something different from what they are in the real world. It was not unusual for my younger daughter, at age two, to hold a banana up to her ear and say "Hullo?", then hand me the 'telephone', insisting that 'Mormor', her maternal grandmother, was on the line. Psychologists call this *object substitution*, and we know it to be one of the earliest forms of make-believe observable in small children.

Pretend play usually peaks when children are between three and five years of age. At this stage they can pretend to have a completely different identity and exist in a completely different social situation than they have in real life. They can 'play house' (which the Danes literally call 'playing daddy, mummy and kids') and navigate hierarchical family relations in new ways. Or they can find their inner superhero, defying the laws of physics as they fly through the air throwing fireballs. They can even cease to be human at all, imitating wild or domestic animals such as an obedient dog or a timid little mouse.

Children all over the world engage in pretend play, but their imaginary worlds can be extremely diverse, as they are conditioned by cultural context. Children on the Marquesas Islands, an archipelago in French Polynesia, often pretend to paddle canoes or go hunting and fishing, even though they are playing on dry land. Children in India sometimes dress in colourful garb, pretending to be a child-form of Lord Krishna or a *gopika*, a herdswoman in Indian folklore and religious mythology who takes care of the sacred cows. Children in the Western world often don capes and glittery dresses to imitate superheroes, princesses and comic-book characters.

There are also differences in the timing and frequency of such play in different cultures. In most Western societies, parents, educators and teachers of small children widely encourage pretend play, but this is not the case everywhere. For example, in Mayan villages on Mexico's Yucatán Peninsula, children of all ages are expected to help out with farm work when they are not at school. Here, adults generally consider play to be a waste of time and expect children to give priority to their domestic duties. Pretend play in particular is discouraged, because it runs counter to a cornerstone of the local value system: to never tell lies, not even for fun. Children in this culture therefore rarely have access to fiction or comic books, which are also regarded as intentionally untruthful.

Despite this adult disapproval, children in the Yucatán nevertheless pretend, although their pretend play does not peak until age six to eight. It seems, then, that the instinct to play is like an unstoppable locomotive – think Thomas the Tank Engine with a vengeance – which will eventually break through any barrier adults try to build against it.

EINSTEIN AND NINJAS

According to the American philosopher and developmental psychologist Alison Gopnik, children prioritise pretend play because it enables them to test a range of hypotheses about how the world works, much like scientists. When toddlers seek new information by squashing Mama's lipstick or tasting Dada's shampoo, they do so because they want to test whether their current theory about lipsticks or shampoo bottles is correct.

Children often discover that their hypothesis is wrong: "No, shampoo tastes awful, so it is probably not food after all." Based on the results of these sometimes unpleasant experiences, they must work out new hypotheses. But what does this process really entail?

For scientists, coming up with a new hypothesis takes more than just a good idea. They must also be able to predict what ought to happen in an experiment if their hypothesis is correct. In the early 1900s, the German-American physicist Albert Einstein formulated his general theory of relativity, which predicts that all bodies with mass will warp or curve space. According to his calculations, very large bodies, such as stars, will curve space so much that rays of light passing them will visibly bend their trajectory. In these cases, Einstein hypothesised that light would travel in a curve around a star rather than going straight past it.

Einstein knew his hypothesis could be tested during a solar eclipse, in locations where stars could be viewed from Earth while the eclipsed Sun was in the sky. Given a star known to be positioned *behind* the Sun during the eclipse, an observer ought to be able to see that star from Earth because its emitted light would travel in a curve around the eclipsed Sun.

During a solar eclipse on 29 May 1919, the British astronomer Arthur Eddington confirmed Einstein's hypothesis and instantly made him world famous. But remember: Einstein first had to formulate what ought to happen if his general theory of relativity was correct. Only then could he design an experiment to test his hypothesis.

When a toddler gleefully flings a fistful of spaghetti carbonara at the dining-room wall, most parents may have a hard time seeing any obvious likeness to Einstein. Nevertheless, it is the same principle at work. Children test their own hypotheses about what consequences their experiments ought to bring about, provided their hypotheses are correct. Bodies with mass curve space; spaghetti in sauce slides down walls.

This approach becomes highly evident in pretend play. Think of my daughter, who at five used to cast me as a despicable supervillain and herself as a heroic, stealthy expert ninja. Soundlessly, she would sneak up on me while I was doing the dishes, then ambush me with a shout and a flurry of kung fu chops and shin kicks. Of course, she knew that she was not really a ninja, and that I was not really a villain. Pretending nevertheless gave her the opportunity to test a number of hypotheses about what would happen if she really *were* a ninja facing an evil arch-enemy.

As in the case of Einstein, pretend play allows children to imagine and test what would happen if their hypothesis about A, B or C were actually correct. In order to do that, children must be able to distinguish reality from an imagined alternative. Psychologists call this *counterfactual thinking* and it is an incredibly important ability for humans to master. Consider the Soviet naval officer Vasili Arkhipov, who, during the Cuban Missile Crisis in 1962, famously refused to fire the atomic torpedo on board his submarine, *B-59*, at the Americans. He refused precisely because he was able to imagine the alternative: nuclear war.

Similarly, directors of national banks can imagine what will happen to the economy of their countries if interest rates are lowered, and parents can imagine the outcome of feeding their children cake for every meal. Likewise, I can imagine what will happen to my marriage if I insist on leaving my sweaty sports clothes on the living room floor instead of tossing them into the laundry basket. In many ways, our success in life – and even the success of humankind as a whole – hinges on our ability to perform counterfactual thinking, which is precisely what children are practising when they pretend.

MIND-READERS

Counterfactual thinking is crucial for our ability to solve problems and learn more about the world, and one of the most vital and interesting problems children and adults face is how to work out what is going on inside the heads of other people. When my wife, calm and poker-faced, says "it's really okay" that I once again forgot our wedding anniversary, I must swiftly deduce that her words do not necessarily match her thoughts – and call the florist immediately.

In psychology, this ability is usually referred to as *theory of mind*: the capacity to infer what is going on in the minds of others. Children gradually develop this skill between age three and five, around the time their pretend play peaks.

When psychologists want to find out how good children are at reading other people's minds, they often use a certain kind of test known as the *false-belief task*. This task tests one's ability to understand that other people can hold false beliefs about the world. The test can be performed in many ways. For instance, an experimenter can show a child a bag of M&M's and ask them to open it. When the child opens the bag – surprise! – it is actually full of marbles instead of tiny chocolates. At this point the experimenter asks, "If your mummy came in to sit with us and saw the M&M's bag, what would *she* think was inside?"

Most three-year-olds incorrectly answer, "Marbles." They cannot yet distinguish between an actual circumstance in the real world – that there are marbles in the bag – and a person's beliefs about the state of the world. However, by age five, most children can correctly deduce that their mother's belief will not match reality. They recognise that she will *think* there are M&M's in the bag, even though the children themselves know that the sneaky experimenter has actually put marbles in the bag.

When children scuttle around on all fours pretending to be the canine heroes Skye, Everest and Chase from the animated television series *PAW Patrol*, the underlying requirements are much like a false-belief test. The children must be able to distinguish between the idea that they are a dog patrol on an important mission, and their identities in the real world. This is why many researchers have long suspected that children's ability to read, or decode, other people's thoughts is closely related to the skills they develop in pretend play. This suspicion has been strengthened by the observation that children with autism spectrum disorders often find it difficult to work out what other people are thinking; these children are also less inclined to engage in pretend play with others than neurotypical children are.

In 1997, this potential link between pretend play and theory of mind was investigated by two American developmental psychologists named Marjorie Taylor and Stephanie Carlson. They designed an experiment in which they divided their sample of three-to-five-year-olds into groups, based on their proficiency in pretend play. Each child was then shown three boxes, one at a time, each with a label visually depicting its contents: Band-Aids, crayons and raisins. However, the labels were deceptive: The children could see that the Band-Aid box actually contained a little toy bear; the crayon box, a little toy horse; and the raisin box, a heart-shaped trinket.

Taylor and Carlson then introduced the children to Chris – a hand puppet none of the children had seen before – and asked what they thought Chris would think was inside the containers. Among the four-year-olds, the children who were good at pretending showed significantly better test results than children who were less proficient pretenders. In other words, the children who were good at pretending knew that Chris would wrongly think the boxes contained Band-Aids, crayons and raisins, even though the children themselves knew otherwise.

Although more research is needed to establish a clear causal link, Taylor and Carlson's experiment further strengthened the assumption that the skills performed and practised in pretend play are linked to, and perhaps even identical to, the skills children use when trying to read the minds of others. These skills are of great benefit later in life as they navigate the complexities of human social interaction, where reading other people's hearts and minds is an essential element.

PLAYTIME FOR GROWN-UPS

BORING OLD REACTIONARIES

With his 1911 story *Peter and Wendy*, the Scottish author James Matthew Barrie introduced the world to Peter Pan, 'the Boy Who Wouldn't Grow Up' – and who could blame him? The typical adult is serious, responsible, predictable and often something of a pessimist. Who would want to be any of those things? Even at the age of five, my eldest knew that Peter Pan had it all figured out, asking me almost weekly: "Oh Daddy, why do grown-ups always have to be so *boring*?"

Her question was spot on. From a child's perspective, grown-ups are often exceedingly boring. However, we are not necessarily boring all of the time, and on occasion we do actually play. Research on adult play is still fairly limited, but lately the topic has been receiving more attention from scientists. As a matter of fact, some findings show that adults play quite a lot, although this may sound rather paradoxical – because if the primary function of play is to help children become better adults, why do some adults continue to play?

Just like children, adults too are constantly coming up with new hypotheses and new ways of testing them. We may want to confirm our suspicion that the neighbours have a drinking problem by counting the empty beer bottles in their garage. We may check whether the stereo loudspeakers have a loose circuit by taking them apart, or test whether our spouse still loves us by noticing the number of hugs and kisses we get. But why don't adults play as much as children do?

Importantly, adults have already gathered heaps of information about how the world works. Having repeatedly confirmed or rejected innumerable hypotheses, they feel sure that the world works in very particular ways. We know that a bowl of pleasantly hot porridge with sugar and a knob of butter is likely to be edible, not to mention tasty and nourishing. Small children are still testing whether the contents of their breakfast bowl might be suitable as gooey ammunition.

Adults have massive databanks that enable them to navigate effortlessly through everything from breakfasts and birthdays to tea parties and traffic intersections. As adults, we sometimes even pride ourselves on our wealth of wisdom, generously sharing it with any child willing to listen. What most of us do not know, however, is that on the whole, adults are a bunch of boring old reactionaries who often rely on assumptions about the world rather than looking at the actual evidence.

In 2014, the American psychologist Christopher G. Lucas and his colleagues did an experiment with a group of four-year-olds and adults, who were all shown a box-shaped 'machine' built of wood, along with some wooden blocks that were square, circular or triangular. When a participant laid certain blocks, or certain combinations of blocks, on the machine's lid, it would light up.

Lucas divided the participants into two groups, with half the adults and half the children in each group. Both groups then had an initial training phase, where the experimenter showed them how the machine worked.

The first group was shown that the machine did not light up when the experimenter put individual blocks on its lid, but that it did light up when there was a particular *combination* of two geometric blocks. The second group was shown the opposite. Here, the experimenter also put individual blocks or combinations of geometric blocks on the machine, but this time the machine was made to light up only when some very particular blocks were laid on its lid. These blocks made the lid light up, whether they were placed there alone or combined with other blocks.

Both groups then moved on to the experiment's test phase, where the experimenter used a whole new set of blocks. This set included a ball-shaped block, which the participants had not seen before. Once again, the experimenter placed individual blocks or combinations of the blocks atop the machine. In this test phase, the machine never lit up when there was only one block on it, whereas it always lit up when there were two blocks on it.

Meanwhile, the cunning experimenter never placed the ball-shaped block on the machine alone. This gave the participants a problem, because, theoretically, the machine might be activated by the ball-shaped block either alone or in combination with another block.

The researchers wanted to see whether the participants would transfer their knowledge from the training phase to the test phase – the point being that depending on their group, the participants had just learned *either* that the machine was activated by specific combinations of blocks, *or* that it was activated by individual blocks. Now here they were, having to decide whether the new ball-shaped block was activating the machine *alone*, or whether it could only activate the machine because it had been *combined* with another block – even though, theoretically, it was impossible for them to know this for certain.

In both groups, the children used their knowledge from the training phase. The children who had seen individual blocks activate the machine assumed it was the ball-shaped block alone that activated the machine in the test phase. Similarly, the children who had seen unique combinations of blocks activate the machine in the training phase assumed that it was probably the combination of the ball-shaped block and another block that made the machine light up in the test phase.

The reasoning of the adult participants was less logical. Regardless of their training phase, the adults always assumed that it was probably the ball alone that made the machine light up in the test phase. But why? Why did only the children use the evidence from the training phase to understand how the machine worked in the test phase?

The uncomfortable answer is that adults become narrow-minded and inflexible with age. The more knowledge we amass in our lives, the more certain we become that the world works in certain ways. And with the exception of very special objects – such as nuclear missiles that can only be launched by a unique combination of two very particular keys – adults are used to seeing one single thing activate another single thing. We use one key to open our front door. We press one button to switch on our television. We pull on one string to call the nurse from our hospital bed.

The adults in the experiment relied on such assumptions of how the world often works, and this meant they did *not* let themselves be affected by the evidence of how the machine actually worked in the training phase. The children, on the other hand, did not show the same bias; they let themselves be guided by empirical principles, like the good scientists they are.

Adults have learned from experience that testing hypotheses about the *physical* world gives little benefit anymore. This is precisely because long ago – before we became boring – we already thoroughly explored and experimented with how the world works, so we glean little new data from flooding the bathroom, turning a handbag upside down or throwing porridge at the wall. Also, we know from experience who will have to clean up the mess.

Our knowledge makes us sure of the world, but it also makes us rigid. We stop paying attention to new causal links and doing explorative experiments – and humans only play in areas where they remain flexible, want to experiment and still expect to learn new things.

PLAY DATES FOR ADULTS

Adults stop investigating water taps, potted plants and electrical outlets, so how and what do they play? This is a hard question, as play is not always seen as socially acceptable in adults. We generally expect ourselves and each other to be productive, whether at work or at home, and many consider play to be a silly, sometimes irresponsible and ultimately unproductive behaviour.

A friend once told me that he often stands in front of the mirror, pretending to be an internationally acclaimed scientist giving his acceptance speech for the Nobel Prize he just won for his groundbreaking research on play. To some this may sound childish, but actually, when they are alone, many adults will pretend to be famous pop stars or idols, although few dare mention it to other adults for fear of being ridiculed.

For this reason, adults chiefly play with people they already know extremely well and trust implicitly. The American communication researcher R. Kelly Aune and his colleagues did an experiment in 1993 in which adult participants were shown one of two different video recordings of three young male university students. Seated around a table, these men told anecdotes about what had transpired the previous night at a local club, as well as talking about an upcoming American football game they wanted to see.

The three students' conversation was as good as identical in the two videos, but in one version they would also take on the roles of the person they were talking about in a given story. For the football narrative, for instance, in the role-taking video one of the men began to talk like a sports commentator: "And Warren Moon goes in the pocket! He has all the time in the world! The wide receiver is wide open! And Moon fumbles the ball!"

When asked about the friendship of the three students, the participants who had seen the video of them playing the sports commentator and other roles believed the students to be much closer friends, compared to the participants who saw the other version of the video. Instinctively, adults assume that people must have a close friendship or relationship if they dare to play in front of each other.

"I LOVE YOU, PUMPKIN"

Does this mean that partners in long-term relationships play a lot? For their book *The Play Solution*, published in 2002, the American psychologists Jeanette and Robert Lauer interviewed some 300 couples with 15–61 years of matrimony behind them. All interviewees had reported, in advance, that they were happily married, and they agreed that play was an essential part of their relationship – most even ranking it higher than shared humour and sex.

As early as 1981 another American psychologist named

William Betcher had done a similar study, asking a wide range of married couples what they would miss most if their marriage were to dissolve. Most replied they would miss their private jokes, shared banter and playful teasing.

In 1992 the American communication researcher Leslie A. Baxter tried to map how partners in long-term relationships typically play. Often such play is physical, as when I approach my wife just before dinner and invite her to take a tango for two – confidently steering us towards the fishcakes in the frying pan. Another favourite is boardgames – Trivial Pursuit, Settlers, Scrabble or backgammon – which we like to *spille* weekly, so I can *lege* that I am a worthy match for my wife, who will undoubtedly trounce me again. All in good fun, of course.

Partners also play with language, inventing words, concepts and even sentences only they understand. Private terms of endearment like 'pumpkin' or 'honeybun' are classics, and other people often get clever code names: 'Thumper' is that techno-music buff upstairs who is happily married to his subwoofer, and 'the Tornado' is that long-winded colleague with the grinding voice.

Another sort of linguistic play is jovially flirtatious or sexually inviting – like "How about a tango for two, in the shower?" or "OK, I'll put the kids to bed while you slip into something more comfortable … like your birthday suit." There are also playful expressions of affection and love – like pretending to be Cookie Monster from *Sesame Street* and chomping at your partner's head while enthusiastically emitting muffled cries of *"Me eat cookie!"*

Working with colleagues, in the 1980s the American communication researcher Robert A. Bell studied the links between playful language and intimacy in 100 young couples. Bell first asked the partners, separately, to indicate how much they liked or loved their partner, how close they felt to their partner, and the likelihood of their marrying their partner in the future.

The couples were reunited and asked to list as many self-invented words or concepts as possible, the meaning of which only they knew. The study found that couples with the most memories of these expressions also reported loving each other most, feeling closest to each other, and considering themselves most likely to marry each other later.

"HOW YOU DOIN'?"

Play is not only an important component for people in long-term relationships. When we go to clubs, approach someone at the local library or at a social function, or use dating apps like Tinder in our search for potential partners, we are also generally interested in how playful they are. Why is this?

Several researchers have claimed that throughout the evolutionary process of natural selection, playing has been an advantage for human beings. The fact is, playful people are more inclined to investigate the world around them and learn more about it. All else being equal, knowing more about the world is definitely an advantage if you want to stay alive in it.

According to the American anthropologist Gerry E. Chick, however, throughout human evolution play has also provided an advantage in sexual selection, as playful people have found it easier to mate and pair up with partners, thereby passing on their genes.

Chick claims that human males and females tend to look for different traits in their partners. One reason is that women run a greater risk by mating with men than vice-versa. If a man has sex with a woman, in evolutionary terms this is about as close to a bullseye as he can get. The man has optimised his chances of passing on his genes, and theoretically he can simply go on his merry way. The woman, on the other hand, is left with the 'burden of procreation': If she gets pregnant and the stud vanishes, she is stuck with the offspring for many years to come.

According to Chick, this is why women are typically pickier than men when choosing sexual partners, as it is important to find a mate who will stay around and protect them. Conversely, men in this narrative are said to focus on whether a woman is fertile, predisposing them to look for young, healthy females as sexual partners.

But what does mating have to do with play? Again according to Chick, males *and* females notice how playful a potential partner is because this particular trait can give them important information, from an evolutionary angle, about their choice of that person as a sexual partner. A playful male signals non-aggression, indicating he is no danger to the female or their potential offspring, given that an invitation to play is, by definition, a promise that no one will get hurt. Inversely, a playful female manifests as young, healthy and fertile, given that playful behaviour chiefly occurs in young, healthy individuals.

Theories like these, based on evolutionary psychology, are extremely difficult to test empirically because playful traits in humans have developed over hundreds of thousands of years. This is also why many scientists call such explanations 'just-so stories', referring to Rudyard Kipling's classic nonsensical fables that explain, among many other mysteries, how the leopard got his spots. Chick has nevertheless found some empirical support for his theories by asking more than 250 American college students to rate 16 different characteristics of their ideal partner. His findings showed that irrespective of gender, respondents gave caring, understanding, intelligent partners high ratings, but they also ranked playfulness and a good sense of humour among a potential partner's most attractive personality traits.

CREATIVITY AND INNOVATION

BRAWN IS GOOD, BUT BRAINS ARE BETTER

In 2017 the Museum of Natural History in Aarhus, my city, opened an evocative exhibition about the animals of the Ice Age, complete with life-sized reconstructions of the European sabre-toothed tiger, the cave bear and the woolly mammoth, all set in a dusky ambience.

As I wandered through the exhibition with my wife and daughters, our five-year-old asked, wide-eyed, where these animals lived. I explained that none of them lived anywhere anymore because they were all extinct. Unfortunately this did not make them any less intimidating, and she and her two-year-old sister stayed close during the half hour it took us to bravely wend our way through the towering displays.

At the museum it struck me how amazing it is that humans have been able to survive while sabre-toothed felines, cave bears and mammoths have been relegated to the pages of dusty textbooks on prehistory. We have neither fur nor large bodies to keep us warm, and nothing at all in the way of fearsome teeth, sharp claws or long tusks for hunting and self-defence.

Besides our opposable, primate-style thumbs, only one thing gives humans any significant advantage over the rest of the animal kingdom: our brains. In this department we leave all other species in the dust. The advantage lies in our unmatched capacity for observing, learning and conceiving new ideas, paired with an almost insatiable urge to socialise with other humans to share our thoughts and knowledge.

The human brain is the key to our supremacy on Earth. We have organised societies based on the efficient division of labour – butchers, bakers, candlestick-makers and myriad other occupations. We have come up with abstract means of payment – cowrie shells, dollars, euros and bitcoins – to avoid bartering with unwieldy goods like cattle and grain. We have invented nifty technologies ranging from the practical to the unfathomable – the wheel, knitting needles, dishwashers, automatic milking systems, mobile phones and space rockets.

Humans are creative, innovative creatures with a seemingly unlimited ability to develop new systems, products and ideas to solve some of our most pressing problems. And in today's globalised world, humanity needs this more than ever.

For businesses, innovation is vital, as new products enable them to capture market shares faster, satisfy customers better and, obviously, make more money. International bodies like the United Nations are equally interested in creativity and innovation as means to promote their work.

In 2015, the UN proposed an ambitious agenda for the future: 17 Sustainable Development Goals (SDGs) that it is urging its 193 member states to support in a coordinated effort the likes of which the world has never seen. The mission: to eradicate poverty, hunger and gender inequality; to promote health, justice and economic growth; and to massively improve sustainability and combat climate change. Addressing these SDG issues, which affect populations worldwide, will require an unprecedented level of creativity and innovation. Play could be part of the solution, as much suggests that play and innovation are intimately linked.

PIZZAFISH AND PENICILLIN

The essence of creativity is breaking fixed patterns and putting things together in new ways. In this sense creativity and play are very similar. Once again, take my daughter, who held up her new box of markers and gave me an offer I couldn't refuse: "Daddy, do you want a tattoo on your arm? Okay, I'll just draw you a tattoo then … See, I'll draw a triangle first, for a tail. No, it really looks a bit like a slice of pizza, Daddy. So Daddy, do you want me to draw a fish, or a pizza? You know what – I could draw a pizzafish?! First the tail … then the body … then lots of pepperoni on top."

The pizzafish may not gain a worldwide following any time soon, but it exemplifies a creative product: It breaks an established pattern, and it joins two domains – live fish and pepperoni pizza – in a way that millions of pizza chefs and fishmongers have not yet envisioned.

Creativity researchers also point out that creativity, like play, primarily occurs when we are in a good mood, and that many of history's most creative people have been exceptionally playful. A shining example is the Austrian composer Wolfgang Amadeus Mozart, who reportedly enjoyed playing music backwards. In 1786/87 he also composed a three-voice canon called 'Difficile lectu', the lyrics of which were nonsensical Latin that came out sounding like obscene phrases in German.

In 1945 an interviewer asked the Scottish physician Alexander Fleming, who famously discovered the effects of penicillin, about the nature of his work. The good doctor explained: "I play with microbes. There are, of course, many rules in this play, and a certain amount of knowledge is required before you can fully enjoy the game, but, when you have acquired knowledge and experience, it is very pleasant to break the rules and to be able to find something that nobody had thought of."

Nowadays the American tech giant Google even encourages its software engineers to spend 20% of their workday on projects they think are fun. This has brought about tangible results, which Google's shareholders no doubt enjoy seeing on the company's bottom line. Innovations include Google News, which helps individual users access news in a tailored format, and Gmail, which has more than 1.5 billion users. Google's policy is sound, given that autonomy, playful interaction with others and a relaxing work environment are all factors that facilitate creativity, as documented in several scientific studies.

THE DAWN OF WHISTLEBLOWING

When we think about inventions and innovation in general, we are inclined to assume that the various types of available entertainment – toys, games, devices – depend on how technologically advanced our culture is. For instance, most would claim that we have our high-tech society to thank for our ability to play computer games like World of Warcraft, Minecraft and Fortnite.

A society's level of technical sophistication certainly determines what we, its natives, can play with, and which objects we use. However, according to the American media theorist Steven Johnson, the causality could be precisely the opposite. In his book *Wonderland: How Play Made the Modern World*, published in 2016, Johnson describes how it is actually our desire to play and have fun that incredibly, unpredictably changes our society.

Humans invented flutes over 40,000 years ago, and archaeologists have unearthed numerous specimens fashioned from cave bear, mammoth and vulture bones. The fact that such ancient ancestors crafted objects with no other apparent purpose than entertainment is, in itself, remarkable.

But there is more. Chronicling the history of the flute, Johnson recounts how, more than 2,000 years ago, others rethought the concept of the flute, arranged a series of pipe-shaped whistles next to each other by size, blew air through them and – *voilà* – the pipe organ was born. Later, someone else had the brilliant idea of arranging the organ pipes' valve activators along a piece of wood – a keyboard – giving rise to new types of instruments, including the harpsichord, piano and grand piano, which all use a keyboard to produce sound.

The mid-1800s brought the idea that keys could also be used to transfer letters to paper using an inked ribbon. This became the typewriter. One of the first of its kind, designed by the Italian inventor Giuseppe Ravizza, was actually called 'the writing harpsichord' or 'the machine that writes with keys'.

About a thousand years ago, three brothers in Baghdad invented a machine which, at the time, they called 'the instrument that plays by itself'. Like the flute, their machine was designed purely for entertainment. It worked along the same lines as a modern-day music box, where a cylinder with precisely placed metal pins revolves and creates a sound pattern, for instance by striking the teeth of a tuned metal comb.

Yet the revolution that lay in 'the instrument that plays by itself' was not its engineering, but the idea to which it gave birth. Just as we can make little music boxes play different melodies by replacing the cylinder, the brothers in Baghdad offered users of their machine an option to change its melody, simply by changing the machine's parameters. This was the first time in history the idea of *programmability* was introduced. Suddenly, people were able to think conceptually in terms reminiscent of today's software and hardware.

In the 1700s, music-making machines became the height of fashion among Europe's upper class. One of the most famous music machines was created by the French inventor Jacques de Vaucanson: a mechanical flute-player that could play 12 different melodies, its fingers activated by a cylinder with metal pins, just like 'the instrument that plays by itself' and modern-day music boxes.

Later, Vaucanson attempted to revolutionise the French textile industry by transferring the principle of cylinder programmability to a loom. Instead of activating musical tones, the cylinder would select variously coloured threads. He ended up creating the world's first automated loom, using a cylinder with metal pins and long paper cards with holes punched in them to control the hooks that selected the threads.

Vaucanson's loom never caught on, mainly because the cylinders were too expensive to make. But in the early 1800s, the French weaver and merchant Joseph Marie Charles dit Jacquard refined Vaucanson's idea by using only punched paper cards to program a pattern on the loom, which was much cheaper than using metal cylinders. It was this idea of 'punch cards' that inspired the English engineer Charles Babbage to design his 'analytical machine' – the world's first actual computer – in 1837.

Unfortunately, Babbage could not obtain funding for his research, and work on his invention stood still for the next hundred years. However, Babbage's design was a central element in the technological development of computing machines, and computer programmers still used punch cards until the mid-1970s.

The traditional story of 'the world's first computer' is rather different, though: During World War II, a secret centre under the British Army, with a group led by the English mathematician Alan Turing, designed the first computer in the quest to crack encrypted Nazi transmissions. According to Johnson this story is not untrue, but he points out that the building of the Turing computer, and computers in general, relied on a whole series of fundamental building blocks that go back much farther than the 1940s: music boxes, key-operated instruments, mechanical flute-players and patterned woven fabric.

Evidently, a variety of other world-changing ideas and inventions were also born out of humankind's natural fondness for play and fun. Originally, around 1500–400 BCE, rubber was used to make balls among the Olmec, the oldest known culture in Meso-America. Today, rubber is a key component in all sorts of objects, from condoms to balloons to car tyres. And probability theory, which today controls everything from apps to military tracking systems, originated in games of chance. As Johnson reasons, if we really want to know where the world's next big breakthrough is going to happen, we ought to fix our eyes on "wherever people are having the most fun."

THE DEMISE OF CLASSIC PLAY

Researchers agree that play is fundamentally a beneficial, healthy activity, but in the Western world the sight of children playing in public spaces has become increasingly rare over the last century. For one thing, modern parents increasingly discourage children from activities like tree-climbing and unsupervised outdoor play. We are afraid they will get hurt. Due to urbanisation and heavier traffic, we also keep children indoors more.

The second thing putting classical forms of play under pressure is intense competition from television and, in recent decades, computers, tablets and smartphones, reducing play with building blocks and construction sets, as well as rope-jumping and hide-and-seek. The surge in child interaction with screens and devices also means that children now play more in their own homes, physically isolated from their friends and peers.

Thirdly, in many countries, including Denmark, children are spending more time at school than ever before, and play in the classroom is still considered a distraction in many places if it takes place during teaching. What is more, in many Western schools, pupils' traditional breaks during the day – spent outside playing ball or hop-scotch, clapping and dancing – have been shortened to allow for more time in class. And overall, longer school days mean fewer hours for children to play.

You may be asking: So what? Surely it is good that our children do not break their arms and legs; that they acquire digital competence; that they go to school and learn the skills they need to get by in life and to get a job?

When researchers test the IQ of large groups of people around the world, we can see people generally becoming smarter every year. In other words, it seems like going to school actually works, so perhaps there is no reason to worry about children playing less. At any rate, our standard battery of assessment tools indicate that children are learning well despite less play time. However, according to Kyung Hee Kim, an American professor of creativity and innovation, our children and societies may be paying the price elsewhere: in lost creativity.

Like play, creativity is very difficult to measure, but a tool called the Torrance Test has been developed in an attempt to do just that. In solving a series of simple tasks, participants score and add up points for their creativity. For example, in one task the participant is given the name of a certain object, then asked to think of smart and unusual ways in which it could be used. A child might be asked to think about what they could use a teddy bear for, besides playing with or hugging. A creative answer might be: a pillow, or a secret hollowed-out stash for goodies.

Originally devised by the American psychologist Ellis Paul Torrance for an experimental study in 1966, the Torrance Test has since been used for five large-scale studies between 1974 and 2008, assessing the creativity of more than 270,000 American children and adults, all told. And in fact, creativity scores since 1990 show a trend opposite to the increasing IQs. As measured by the

Torrance Tests, it would seem that people are becoming less and less creative.

Also according to Hee Kim, over this period children have become less verbally and emotionally expressive, less energetic and lively, less humorous, less imaginative, less unconventional and less likely to see things from different angles. She has proposed several explanations for this. Perhaps the findings are due to tech-intensive lifestyles reducing children's scope and frequency of social interaction, the context in which many of these qualities are often exercised.

Or perhaps they are due to the way schools, not least in the US, increasingly focus on rote learning and standardised tests at the expense of critical, reflective, creative problem solving, and subjects like language, music and art. Hee Kim also points out that limited opportunities to play at school and at home could be adversely affecting children's creativity scores. Play gives children opportunities to try out new solutions and ideas – an essential part of any creative process.

IN SEARCH OF SURPRISE

Play is a complex phenomenon that comes in an endless variety of shapes and sizes. My own research investigates whether, despite this infinite diversity, there may be some general principle found across all forms of play; some common denominator, identifiable regardless of age, cultural background or activity, whether or not it involves porridge ammunition, banana phones or decrees from the sovereign, coconut-water-slurping princess of Atecopia.

In recent years, researchers in cognitive neuroscience have discovered that the human brain works like a sort of advanced prediction machine that constantly tries to predict or guess what the future will bring. It can do this because it gathers information throughout our lives about the various probabilities of how the world might work in certain situations.

By relying on this prior knowledge, the brain is able to get things right most of the time. For instance, at the front door of an unfamiliar house, we instinctively push it because we expect front doors, as such, to open inwards. This strategy of forming expectations on the basis of prior knowledge is quite clever, because it allows the brain to act quickly and expend a minimum of energy doing so.

Thanks to this economical principle, the brain only seriously wakes up and kicks into action when it makes wrong predictions and is surprised. When this happens, it registers 'prediction errors', which it does not like at all. To make these nasty signals disappear, the brain has to change and update its knowledge about the world, making its surroundings predictable once again. Therefore, it is precisely during these moments of surprise that we have opportunities to learn new things.

From this perspective of brain function, play becomes an extremely interesting form of behaviour for cognitive scientists to investigate, because it fundamentally appears to be a deliberate quest for measured doses of unpredictability. Apparently, when people play they intentionally place themselves in situations where they are constantly making little predictive mistakes. Not *big* mistakes; not *no* mistakes; but a steady flow of small – and manageable – mistakes in their predictions.

It may seem strange that we seek out mistakes and errors on purpose, but this idea is supported by numerous findings in developmental psychology. One is the so-called Goldilocks Principle, which refers to an infant's preference for looking at visual stimuli that are 'just right', in that they offer the appropriate element of surprise.

In the well-known tale of Goldilocks, the little girl decides which porridge bowl at the bear family's breakfast table to eat from, choosing the one in between: neither too hot nor too cold, but just right. In the same fashion, play lets children discover new information that is neither too complex nor too simple, but just right.

Perhaps the prediction-machine framework could also explain why children prefer playmates their own age, with interests similar to their own. Such predictable playmates seem ideal for sharing and containing the unpredictable practice of play.

It could also explain why play is so enormously versatile and has such universal appeal. A water tap can give a two-year-old child a constant flow of small surprises, whereas a five-year-old might find its predictable drips and sprays about as exciting as watching paint dry. In much the same way, some phenomena can be mildly surprising to one five-year-old but utterly predictable to another, depending on prior experience.

In other words, play is highly dependent on what we know and what we do not. When we play, we explore the borderlands of our extant sphere of knowledge. Totally unpredictable play is not very fun; it is chaotic. Predictable play is not fun either; it is boring. But when we find the sweet spot, the perfect path through our personal borderlands, it feels just right, playful and fun! And the playful quest for perfectly dosed surprise is also an extremely effective learning strategy for children, because it solves the dilemma that highly predictable events are devoid of information, whereas highly unpredictable events take large amounts of energy to process.

The same may well apply to adults. In an experiment conducted in 2017 by Katrin Heimann and Andreas Roepstorff – two of my colleagues at the Interacting Minds Centre at Aarhus University – 22 participants each received five little plastic bags. Each bag contained six Lego bricks in various sizes. Four were yellow and two were red, and one of the yellow bricks had an eye on opposing sides.

Using these bricks, the participants could build a small duck, making the eye-brick into the head, for instance, and using the flat, red bricks for the beak and feet, with the other bricks becoming the body. In fact, the six little Lego bricks could be combined in more than 13 million different ways, giving the participants ample opportunity to build many other models of a duck. I should also mention that since many of the test subjects were born and raised in Denmark – the home of Lego – they would most likely have been proficient builders, intimately acquainted with the bricks from an early age.

In the experiment, Heimann asked participants to build five ducks across two rounds, ten ducks in all. In one round, the participants were asked to build the ducks in a way that felt playful to them; in another round, in a way that did *not* feel like playing. The effect of the playful mindset was striking. The researchers found that participants were far more likely to build lots of different ducks when they felt playful, whereas many just built the same duck over and over again in the round where they did not feel playful.

After the experiment Heimann interviewed the participants. When describing the playful round, they emphasised 'autonomy' and 'surprise' as key elements in their play experience. They also reported that in the playful round they somehow managed to arrive at a building style that surprised them when they looked at their final duck models. And that is not all. Their surprise at their own ability to come up with novel-looking ducks made them feel more competent, motivating them to want to build even *more* ducks that were even more novel and surprising.

If play entails a steady flow of small surprises, that might explain why play and creativity seem to be so closely linked. By definition, creativity produces a surprising result: an object, idea or arrangement that no one has thought of before.

Now imagine what happens when engineers, astrophysicists, doctors, educators, composers, programmers, designers, architects and researchers place themselves in situations where they are able to produce one surprising result after another, on the cutting edge of their already specialised knowledge. Might this make play the key to the next big, innovative breakthrough?

If we want to be creative and innovative, and to have fun doing it, we could consider spending less time with our eyes glued to purported paragons of innovation like Steve Jobs of Apple, Bill Gates of Microsoft and Elon Musk of Tesla. Instead, we could take a good look around the living room where the real experts are testing their new coloured markers on the wallpaper. You see, children know that their time is best spent breaking rules, trying out new ideas and playfully searching for the next exhilarating dose of surprise.